The Wigwam and
the Longhouse

The Wigwam and the Longhouse

Charlotte and David Yue

HOUGHTON MIFFLIN COMPANY
BOSTON

The text of this book is set in 13-point Goudy.
The illustrations are pen and ink and watercolor.

Library of Congress Cataloging-in-Publication Data
Yue, Charlotte.
The wigwam and the longhouse / Charlotte and David Yue.
p.   cm.
Summary: Describes the history, customs, religion, government, homes, and present-day status
of the various native peoples that inhabited the eastern woodlands since before the coming of
the Europeans.
ISBN 0-395-84169-0
1. Woodland Indians — Juvenile literature.   [1. Woodland Indians. 2. Indians of North
America — Northeastern States.] I. Yue, David. II. Title.
E78.E2Y84   2000
973'.04973 — dc21   98-28971 CIP AC

Manufactured in the United States of America
MV 10 9 8 7 6 5 4 3 2

For sisters,
especially Jeanne Bustard and Louise Gribling

Contents

CHAPTER ONE

The People & the Land

The People Who Lived in the Eastern Woodlands

Before white men came to America, deep forests covered most of the northeastern part of the land. Woodlands stretched from the Atlantic Ocean across the Appalachian Mountains to the Mississippi River Valley and from Newfoundland and southern Canada to Virginia and North Carolina. Rising columns of smoke from campfires marked the villages of lodges huddled near winding rivers or clear lakes.

The people who lived in these villages were strong and tall. Their average height was greater than that of most Europeans at the time of their first encounter. They had dark eyes and dark, straight hair. Over countless generations, they had observed and studied their surroundings. The people developed a system that enabled them to grow crops successfully and to take advantage of the myriad of resources as they became available.

Their code of behavior encouraged qualities that supported the system and made people better at carrying out their jobs. Courage, endurance, daring, and self-control were essential traits for men as hunters and warriors. Patience, hard work, and thrift were important for women as farmers and housekeepers. Since people lived and worked close together as a community, they were expected to show thoughtfulness, hospitality, and honesty toward one another. Old people were highly respected. Their experience and advice were valuable to hunters and warriors, as well as to farmers. Older women were often needed to care for small children while their mothers worked in the fields or foraged in the woods. Cruelty and deception toward enemies strengthened the tribe in the eyes of neighboring people, who learned to fear them and keep a respectful distance away.

Building houses and villages was a communal effort. Everyone shared the responsibilities and the space in their homes and their villages, but each person had his or her own place and jobs. People shared their wealth when things went well and went hungry together when times were hard. The contribution of each individual was important and necessary for the survival of the group.

Although the woodlands was not as harsh an environment as many others, it took ingenuity and an intimate knowledge of the land to eke out a living. Women knew where to find plants, which ones had nutritional value and which ones were poisonous, the times to harvest them, and how they could be used. Men learned the habits of the animals: where they lived, what they ate, when they slept.

Ceremonies and rituals helped people remember the order, time, and place for work to be done throughout the

Elm   Sugar Maple   Chestnut   White Oak   Red

yearly cycle. Stories and legends were recited and passed on from generation to generation. These stories explained and reinforced the tribe's cultural values.

The woodlands people originated from two groups, the Iroquoians and the Algonquians, which had common bloodlines and language stocks. Over the centuries, bands moved apart and developed their own distinct customs and languages. As time passed, they saw themselves as separate tribes and did not recognize any common bonds. Some groups had become enemies. The descendants of the Iroquoians lived mostly around the St. Lawrence River, Lake Ontario, and Lake Erie. The Algonquians' descendants settled in Nova Scotia, southern Canada, New England, along the Atlantic coast, and in the remaining Great Lakes regions.

The names we know them by today are rarely the names they called themselves. These names usually described where they lived or a notable feature of their tribe. They took names that meant "People of the Island," "People of the Upright Stone," "People on the Mountain," and "People of the Flint." When Europeans encountered these tribes, they often referred to them by names that came from misunderstandings. All native peoples of the Americas are called Indians, the name Columbus used, believing he had reached India. White people gave the tribes names in their own language or adopted disparaging names used by enemies. People who called themselves Wendat, "Dwellers on a Peninsula," were called Huron by the French, using a French term to describe them as "unkempt boors." Iroquois was probably a European adaptation of a name meaning "poisonous snakes" or "killer people," used by their enemies for the Hodenosaunee, or "People of the Longhouse." Eventually, many of these names replaced the real names of the tribes.

Some tribes joined together into confederacies, but most native people saw themselves as separate nations. Most groups built villages in clearings where they farmed a dependable food supply and worked together as a community, but they also made seasonal expeditions into the forest to take advantage of the plant and animal life there. House forms, clothing designs, food, ways of making weapons and tools, hairstyles, pottery styles, ornaments, and religious beliefs and ceremonies varied from tribe to tribe.

The forest was central to the lives of all the people. It held the plants and animals that supplemented the food they grew. The woodland also provided materials for homes, canoes, clothing, and tools. The native people viewed themselves as part of the forest community rather than its masters. Their religious and cultural beliefs expressed a deep reverence for the land, a kinship with all wildlife, and a wish to live within the balance of nature. As part of this community, they believed that humans must share the resources with all earth's creatures, take only what was needed, and not be wasteful. The Indians used the resources of the forest to survive, but they used them in ways that ensured the survival of the resourses as well. Descendants of these people continue to hold many of the same beliefs today.

What the Woodlands Were Like before the White Men Came

Although the Northeast has become one of the most industrialized and densely populated areas in the United

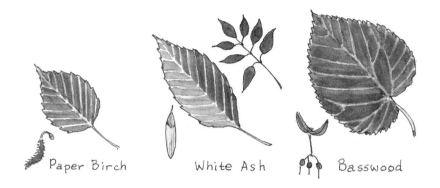

Paper Birch   White Ash   Basswood

States, when it was the country of the Woodlands Indians, it was a beautiful and varied landscape of mountains and valleys, winding rivers and steep waterfalls, lakes and sea-coast. The most outstanding feature of the land was the forest. Much of the region seemed to be one immense, uninterrupted forest, which extended from river to river, lake to lake. Trees covered mountains and valleys and stretched along the coast, growing down to the ocean's edge. A squirrel could leap from tree to tree for a thousand miles without having to touch the ground. Deep green coniferous forests of pine, fir, spruce, and hemlock in the northern parts of the woodlands blended into the decidu-ous forests to the south—forests of maple, chestnut, oak, birch, beech, elm, ash, and basswood, which flamed with color in the fall.

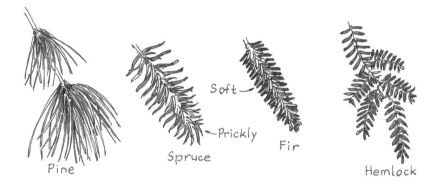

Pine

Spruce

Soft

Prickly

Fir

Hemlock

The forest was a dark, quiet world, dimly lit by shafts of light that filtered down through the interlocking branches overhead. The people walked among huge columns of trees, bare of branches except far up at the top. The cries of birds and the skittering of animals would suddenly break the silence. The forest was home to deer, bears, beavers, squirrels, porcupines, wild turkeys, and grouse. Eels and salmon swam in the streams, and trout, bass, and sturgeon filled the ponds and lakes.

Although the forest was immense, there were many open spaces. The people found that the clearings had fertile soil, easily worked with tools made of stone, wood, or bone. There was plenty of rainfall and, in most parts of the region, enough days without frost to cultivate crops. There was a regular succession of seasons. The summer was long and warm enough for growing maize, the Indians' corn. The winters were not too severe. Woodlands people divided their lives between the forest and the clearing, taking advantage of nature's bounty in both.

CHAPTER TWO

Patterns of Time and Space

In the clearings, the Woodlands Indians built their villages and farmed their land. The forest was stocked with a wealth of plants and animals to supply their daily needs. Each season brought its materials and foods to be gathered and prepared for use. Some of this work took place in the clearing, some in the forest.

The forest provided wild food—birds, fish, animals, roots, berries, and plants. Among the towering trees there was little that had been created by humans. The land stretched toward distant hunts, villages of friends, enemy territories, and unknown places. The Indians believed that the land was also filled with spirits who lived in everything in nature and had the power to control hunting, travel, trade, and war.

The clearing was bright with sunshine and full of the noises of people at work and play. It was a manmade area, with houses and gardens producing domesticated foods— corn, beans, and squash. The settlement was protected by corn spirits. It was a place of safety and security.

The forest and the clearing held two contrasting parts of their lives, both related and both necessary. Life moved back and forth between these two worlds according to the season.

The cycle of time for most woodlands people began in the midwinter, when the earth was sleeping. The weather was cold. Frozen rivers and lakes blended into the land. The forest was icy and still. Birds had flown to warmer climates, and most animals had burrowed away for the winter. As the days grew shorter and the nights longer, the people watched the night sky. When the seven stars of the Pleiades were directly overhead, the people left their hunting campsites and returned to the village in the clearing for the Midwinter Festival.

This was a time to come together as a community, to look back over the past year and prepare for the new year. People stayed close to their fires, only traveling short distances on snowshoes. The crops had been harvested and stored, the fall hunt was over, and there were no wild plants, seeds, roots, or nuts to be gathered. People gave thanks to the Creator for the existence of all things. They gave thanks that all the living things on earth had carried out their responsibilities and asked that they would continue to do so in the coming year. There were games to play and stories to tell. Women sewed clothes, mats, and moccasins and made snowshoes and containers. Men made tools and utensils and repaired nets for fishing.

The earth began to awaken again after the snowy cold of winter. Soon it was the time when the sap rose in the sugar maple. The people left the village and set up smaller camps, where they tapped the trees and gathered the sap. Making maple sugar was a job for the whole family. Men cut gashes in the trees and fitted pieces of shaped wood in them. The sap ran down the wood and dripped into containers. Some people used hollowed-out logs to hold the sap. Others made vessels of birch or elm bark, stitched

Summer
Sugar Maple
Leaf

together with spruce roots or basswood fibers and sealed
with resin. Young boys guarded the pans, keeping away
squirrels, rabbits, and the other small animals that tried to
gnaw holes in the bark containers or knock them over.
The thin, sweet sap was boiled down into syrup and made
into sugar. Men helped boil the sap. The Indians did not
have large pots that could withstand the heat of a fire, so
they heated stones until they were red-hot and placed

them in the syrup. The thickened syrup was hardened in bark molds or eggshells and stored in rawhide or bark pouches.

As the days grew warmer, women gathered the first spring vegetables—young shoots of cattails and fronds of ferns—and collected wild onion bulbs to use for flavoring.

Soon after sugaring time, returning birds filled the skies. Flocks of wild pigeons were so enormous, they blocked out the sunlight. Again the people left the village to hunt the nesting birds and gather eggs. At night, when the birds roosted on branches of trees, people knocked them off with sticks.

Another event of early spring was the run of fish swimming upstream to spawn. People from different tribes gathered at waterfalls and rapids, where migrating fish were forced to slow down. Shad, salmon, sturgeon, and herring were speared by the thousands. Some people built weirs of stone or woven branches reaching out from opposite banks of rivers and streams. As the fish headed into the narrow passage, they could be dipped out with nets. Nets took a long time to make but were worth the effort. Indians used large nets as well as hand-held scoop nets.

The taste of fresh fish cooked over the fire was especially welcome after the dried food of the winter. Some fish were smoked, to be brought back to the village and stored, and some were used for fertilizer when the planting season began.

Women knew it was time for planting when oak leaves had grown to the size of a squirrel's ear. The soil would be thawed and warmed and ready to receive seeds. Men helped clear the land for farming, an ongoing project that was accomplished over many seasons. Large trees were girdled by pounding a deep groove around the trunk with a stone ax. This treatment usually stopped the flow of sap and killed the tree. Sometimes the dead tree could be left standing, allowing sunlight to shine on the crops through the bare branches. If the man needed to remove the tree, he would chop it down with his ax or pile brush around the trunk and set it on fire. Grass, brush, insects, and weeds were sometimes cleared from the fields by burning. Besides getting rid of unwanted vegetation, burning helped with fertilization. The ashes loosened the soil and made it more workable, and the elimination of surface cover gave the new crop maximum sunlight with little competition from other plants. Some people spread brush over barren places and set it on fire to make the land productive again.

Before planting, women soaked the seeds from the past harvest in warm water. Work parties of women and children took their seeds to the fields surrounding the village. Laughing and joking as they worked, the women prepared the earth with hoes. The blade of the hoe was made from a large animal bone, wood, shell, or stone. Then, using a straight, pointed digging stick, they made holes a few inches deep and about three or four feet apart. Some women put two or three fish in each hole as fertilizer and covered them with soil. Then they put in the seeds. Maize, the Indians' corn, and beans were planted in the same hole—four maize and two bean seeds. Pumpkins and other squash were planted between them. Cornstalks would serve as beanpoles, and the broad leaves of the squash helped keep out weeds.

The newly planted fields needed careful guarding for the next two weeks. Birds would try to eat the seeds, and dogs and other animals were attracted by the fish. Sometimes the women tried soaking the seeds in a mixture containing hellebore, a plant used in some medicines. Birds that ate these seeds became dizzy and frightened away other thieves. After the plants began to grow, women piled up the soil to form a base around them.

In late spring, tiny wild strawberries appeared in the woods, and women and girls went to gather them. Everyone enjoyed the sweet taste of these first fruits of the year. Women and children also picked mulberries and juneberries. Some were eaten fresh, others dried and stored. Late spring was also when the men peeled bark from elm and birch trees for houses and canoes.

The corn grew tall during the hot summer days. The women weeded their fields, went fishing, and made short expeditions into the woods to replenish their supplies of plants for vegetables, dyes, and medicines and to collect reeds and bark to weave into mats and containers. Strawberries, raspberries, blueberries, and wild cherries were

gathered during the summer. Soon the first beans and squash were ready to eat.

While the women worked in the clearing, the men hunted and fished in the forest. Men and boys maintained traps and deadfalls to catch small game in the woods around the settlement. This helped keep animals from raiding the crops. Since these animals had many uses besides providing food, the men designed their traps to prevent damage to the skin and fur as well as to keep the captured animal from gnawing its way out. A deadfall had a weight triggered to drop when sprung by the animal, either pinning or killing it. The pitfall was a concealed trap into which the creature fell. Snares and nooses were also set to trap animals.

When the first ears of corn were ripe and ready to eat, the village held a festival. No one ate any of the corn until the first ear was offered to the gods in thanks. Then the feasting, games, and dancing could begin.

Late summer was the time to harvest wild rice growing in the shallow waters along streams and lakes. Women worked in pairs. Before the grain was ripe, one woman would steer the canoe while the other bound the stalks into bundles. This prevented the ripe grains from being scattered by the wind and eaten by birds. The women returned when the rice was ready to be harvested. While one women poled the canoe, the other pulled the bundles over and knocked the rice into the canoe with a stick. The rice was then brought back to the village to be prepared for use.

Soon the cornstalks were changing from green to yellowish-brown. The leaves on the forest trees were turning brilliant shades of red, orange, and gold. It was time for the harvest, one of the busiest times of the year. The people worked together, gathering the corn, beans, pumpkins, and squash and bringing them to the village before the first frost. Corn was husked, braided, and hung to dry. Some was pounded into meal. Late-ripening blackberries, sweet crabapples, and cranberries were harvested from the woods. They dug pits in which they kept a stock of food for the winter. The storage pits were lined with bark, clay, or stones and preserved food well without freezing. A good harvest assured the people that they would have food for the long winter ahead.

Now the nights were growing longer and the days were

crisp and cool. It was time for the fall hunt. Autumn was the most important hunting season because the meat would not spoil as readily in the cold weather. Most of the people packed the things they needed into bags and baskets and went into the forest. The women and girls set up temporary camps of small huts. They built sapling frames and covered them with the rolls of mats they carried. While the men and boys hunted, the women gathered the nuts, roots, and plants of autumn. Nuts and seeds were eaten raw, ground into flour, or used as a source of oil. Roots could be eaten like potatoes, added to soups, or made into flour.

Mornings and evenings were the best times to hunt ducks and geese. Men would go into the marshes and drift quietly in their canoes to where the birds settled at night. Then the men lit torches. The sudden light caused confusion among the birds, and the hunters knocked them down with their paddles. Dogs were sometimes trained to jump into the water and retrieve the game.

The bow and arrow was the chief weapon used for hunting, though spears and slings were also used. Sometimes the men worked together to drive animals into the water, where waiting hunters could shoot them. Some-times they drove a herd of animals between a converging pair of barriers into a timber and brush corral.

Other hunting techniques involved stalking animals. Putting on animal horns and skins, a hunter would approach the animal from downwind so he would not be detected until he was within bowshot. Some men could imitate the call of the turkey or other birds so well that they were able to move in close enough to capture them. Sometimes a hunter would mimic the cry of a fawn, hop-ing to attract a doe, or he would rub something against a tree to copy the sound a female made to call a buck.

Hunting parties often traveled great distances from the campsite, staying in the forest for days. Hunters sometimes used fires to clear spaces so they could travel more easily and quietly and to make the game more visible. They

burned the withered grass and the dried leaves of autumn, eliminating underbrush and leaving larger, more fire-resistant trees unharmed. Fire might also be used to drive game for large, organized kills.

Indians used fire, to some extent, to create game parks. Burning left more open country and produced an abundance of grass, shrubs, and herbs. This nutritious food supply attracted large populations of deer. Blueberries and acorn-bearing oak trees also grew better in areas cleared by fire and brought heath hens, turkeys, and the other animals that fed on them. Concentrating game on the burned sites minimized the amount of time, energy, and effort spent hunting and helped keep animals away from the village fields.

When the kill was brought back to the hunting camp, the venison or other meat would be cooked and eaten fresh. If the hunt had been good, there would also be enough meat to dry and store for later use. Women prepared the hides, which could later be fashioned into clothes, blankets, and coverings. Bones were crafted into tools and implements. Sinews were used for cordage.

Some people went to coastal campsites. They lived in

small huts and built sheds for smoking oysters, crabs, clams, and scallops. Inland tribes would trade deer and other food and equipment for shellfish. When families returned to the village or moved to a new campsite, they packed their belongings and rolled up the mats covering the wigwams, leaving the bare frames. People generally returned to the same seasonal campsites. Often they could just use or repair the old frames and put on the covering.

As the weather turned colder and snow fell on the hunting camps, people told stories around the fire in the long evenings. Many woodlands people believed that it was safe to tell stories only when the birds and animals would not be tempted from their tasks to listen. As the position of the moon and stars told them the time for the Midwinter Festival was approaching, the hunting parties returned to the villages.

CHAPTER THREE
The Wigwam

The People Who Lived in Wigwams

Throughout the woodlands, there was one basic architectural form—a structural framework of saplings with a covering of bark sheets or sewn reed mats. This form was very versatile. Buildings varied in shape, size, and materials, depending on the available resources, the tribe's customs, and the builder's purposes.

This structure was also well suited to the people of this region, who moved from place to place in their seasonal round of activities. Most people lived in more than one campsite during the year. Wigwams could be transported easily since they were made of separate frames and coverings. Saplings for the framework were readily available almost everywhere. Coverings could be rolled up and easily carried. A small hut could be set up in about an hour for overnight shelter, and temporary camps in the woods were erected in several hours. Larger, more permanent houses could be built in the villages. The form could be elongated to house two or more families or made long enough to hold ceremonies or council meetings.

The word "wigwam" comes from an Algonquian word meaning "house." Woodlands people built circular or oval domed wigwams, conical wigwams, and rectangular barrel-roofed and gable-roofed wigwams. The most common form was a round or oblong domed lodge built for one or two families. These wigwams were the homes of the Chippewa, Abenaki, and most Algonquian tribes, but many other Indian groups used the basic structure at some time. Many groups constructed them as seasonal camps and for temporary shelters in the forest. Tribes throughout the country built their sweat lodges using a similar design.

Wigwam Construction

The builder first marked the floor plan on the ground. The wigwam could be a circle or an oval averaging from 7 to 20 feet in diameter. Poles were placed about 2 feet apart, enclosing the floor space. Young saplings from elm, hickory, basswood, or ironwood trees made the best poles. The builders looked for trees that were strong and flexible, ones that bent easily when green and toughened without cracking or splintering when they dried. Sometimes a sapling was split lengthwise to bend it more easily. The thick end

of the pole was usually cut to a point and set in the ground angled outward. The rounded shape formed when the poles were bent inward would help direct rain away from the house. This was also a stronger structural form.

Opposite poles were bent to form a tunnel of arches. They were overlapped and twisted, then tied together, using cord made from the inner bark of basswood or walnut trees. The remaining poles were bent and joined to these arches. Horizontal poles were added for strength, and the whole structure was lashed tightly together. The inside height was about 6 to 9 feet at the center.

Men and women worked together to make the frame. Then the women attached the covering: bark mats, mats of sewn reeds, or a combination of both. Bark sheets were heavier and more awkward to transport than reed mats, so they were usually reserved for more permanent wigwams. When combining both kinds, women placed the reed mats around the walls and draped the bark sheets over the round roof.

Bark was harvested in the spring when the sap was running. Elm and birch were preferred; oak, pine, black ash, hemlock, and chestnut could also be used. Rings were cut

around the tree and strips peeled off the living trees with an ax. Sections of the bark about a yard square were sewn together with spruce root into 9- to 15-foot rolls. A wooden strip was added at each end to keep the mats from tearing, and cords were attached to fasten the mat to the wigwam. After they had been stored for a while, the rolls became stiff and brittle, so they were warmed over a fire until they were pliable.

Cattail stalks and bullrushes for reed mats were cut in late summer or fall. The women soaked the long stalks to soften them and laid them out on the ground for sewing.

Using 10-inch bone needles and spruce root fibers, they sewed the flattened reeds into mats about 4 feet wide and 8 to 10 feet long. The stalks were overlapped and sewn tightly and neatly to keep out the wind and rain; the vertical grain of the reeds helped with the runoff. These mats also had wooden strips at each end and cords for attaching them to the sapling framework.

Beginning at the doorway, the woman unrolled a mat along the base of the frame and tied it to the first horizontal pole. She added other mats to complete the circle. Upper mats overlapped lower ones for drainage and insulation. An 18-inch square was left open at the top to allow smoke to escape. Sometimes the edges were fireproofed with a coating of mud. A small mat adjusted the wind draft and covered the smokehole when it rained.

The doorway was about 3 feet high. A mat, a deerskin, or a piece of bark was attached at the top. Additional door hangings were added in cold weather. If two families shared the wigwam, they often had separate entrances.

Poles were placed against the outside of the lodge to keep the mats in position in windy weather. If the house was to last a long time, men might build an external frame of saplings over the hut.

Living in a Wigwam

After the wigwam was built, the woman set to work on the inside. For a temporary shelter, she would build a fire and arrange sleeping mats on the floor. Belongings could be stored on the floor or hung from frame poles.

If the wigwam was to be occupied for a long time, she tried to make it a comfortable place to live. A platform

Fishing Basket

Birchbark Basket

Elm Bark Bucket

Clay Pot

Burl Bowl

Oak Basket

Wood Bowl

Wood Spoon & Ladles

Birch Scoop

was built around the walls for sitting and sleeping. Forked sticks were arranged to support poles 12 to 18 inches from the ground. Planks were put along the support poles and braced to the house frame. Mats covered the platforms. Skins and furs arranged on the platforms served as blankets and doubled as cloaks. Baskets and belongings were stored under the platform. Tools and other equipment were hung on the walls.

The hearth was built of small stones in the center of the wigwam, and the earthen floor around it was spread

with mats and hides. A fire was kept burning, with the smoke rising through the smokehole. The fire gave heat and light and served as a stove for cooking. Earthenware pots, polished wooden bowls, cooking utensils, ladles, and spoons were kept within easy reach. If the smokehole had to be completely closed, the women avoided a smoky hut by heating stones on a fire outside and bringing them in to serve as radiators.

Additional mats were often fastened to the interior walls. These provided added insulation. They were also decorative, often woven in geometric patterns or painted.

Many people kept dogs. Some were trained to help with hunting and to obey commands. As many as a half dozen of these slim, wolflike animals lived with the family in the wigwam. Sometimes the dogs had their own sleeping place on a platform.

In large wigwams, two or more fires burned along a central aisle. Each hearth was shared by two families. Partitions of mats divided the interior into living areas for each family. People were expected to keep their part of the lodge neat and clean and respect one another's privacy.

The wigwam was usually owned by the oldest female occupant, whose reputation rested on her skills as builder, housekeeper, and proprietor of the house.

A well-made wigwam was a warm and cozy shell. It was pliable, lightweight, and provided effective insulation, a fine house for a mobile people living in varying environments.

CHAPTER FOUR

The Longhouse

The People Who Lived in Longhouses

The longhouse was a large, communal dwelling and, like
the wigwam, had a sapling framework and was covered
with bark sheeting. The families it housed were usually
related through the female head of the household. They
lived there year-round, although families or groups of families would spend some time at their temporary campsites.
The League of the Iroquois, the Huron Confederacy, other
Iroquoians, and the Delaware built longhouses. The dis-
tinction between a large, elongated wigwam occupied by
many families and the longhouse was not always apparent.
A longhouse was usually framed differently. It also held
special cultural significance in the stories and legends of

longhouse people and was a symbol of their solidarity. Houses were not individual statements. People built their houses as their ancestors had before them.

Longhouse Construction

Longhouses averaged from 50 to 150 feet long, 15 to 20 feet high, and 20 to 30 feet wide, but houses 200 feet long were not uncommon. They usually housed thirty to sixty people. Building a house was a communal effort. The floor plan was a long rectangle, sometimes rounded at the ends. The frame was constructed of forked poles set upright into the ground about every 4 feet. The poles were about 3 inches in diameter and set a foot deep. Horizontal crosspoles were fixed in the forks to frame the walls. Slender poles were fastened at the top of each wall post. Opposite poles were bent and tied together at the top to form a separate arched roof. Support poles were sometimes lashed between pairs of wall poles at right angles across the width of the house. Two rows of interior poles defined the central corridor and supported the two platforms that ran down each side of the longhouse.

While Algonquians preferred birch bark for their wigwams, the Iroquoians used elm whenever possible for covering their longhouses, because the elm tree had special significance in their legends. Bark was gathered and prepared in the same way. The thick sheets were tied to the frame, overlapping like shingles, with a doorway left at each end. Square smokeholes were left open along the center of the roof about every 20 feet to accommodate the fireplaces in the house. Longhouses had no windows; smokeholes and doors provided light and ventilation. The bark covering was secured and the structure strengthened with an outside framework of sapling poles.

In some houses, a flat-roofed storage area extended about 12 feet from each end. It held firewood and food supplies in winter. In summer, the bark shingles could be removed from the sides to make a sleeping porch for the children.

Longhouses were usually tall in proportion to their width and varied in length according to the number of fires. The building was periodically enlarged to hold newly married couples. Each new fire added 20 to 25 feet to the

length of the structure. Small bark houses were also built for one or two families. They were usually framed the same way, with straight walls and a separate arched roof.

The Delaware and other people constructed special longhouses for ceremonies. These lodges had ridge poles, which gave the building a straight, pointed roof. After contact with Europeans, these structures and some log cabins began to appear more frequently in native villages. By the late eighteenth century, the traditional barrel-roofed longhouse was a thing of the past.

Living in a Longhouse

A carving or painting of an animal above the door identified the clan of the people living in the longhouse. A carving of a turtle would mean it was the home of people of the Turtle Clan.

The people entered by lifting the bark door and came into a vestibule where stacks of firewood and containers of food and water were stored. The entry opened onto a long corridor about 8 feet wide. The inside of the longhouse

was dark compared to the bright sunlight outside and seemed hazy from the smoke coming from a row of fires. Bowl-shaped hearths were hollowed in the earthen floor about every 20 feet down the center of the corridor to provide heat and light and serve as cooking stoves. Each fire was shared by two families living across the corridor from each other.

Tall poles were used to close the smokeholes when it rained. The smoke and draft were regulated by adjusting the smokehole covers and by opening or closing the bark doors at each end of the house. Parts of the wall coverings could be rolled up or removed to let in light and air.

The space on either side of the aisle was divided into compartments about 13 feet long and 6 feet wide that opened onto the center hall. Each compartment was the private, domestic space for one family, partitioned from the next by bark sheets. There was usually a storage area between the compartments. A high shelf ran the entire length of the building along each side wall. Lower platforms, about a foot or two off the ground, were built along the wall in each compartment to serve as bunks for sitting and sleeping. Mats of woven grass or cornhusks were spread on the bunks, and blankets of deerskins and bear fur could be used on cold nights. Cooking utensils, bowls and spoons, weapons, dried tobacco, and other articles belonging to the family were stored on the floor under the platform. The high platform held more family belongings. Bark containers, baskets, and skin sacks held the family's supply of beans, dried berries, maple sugar, bear grease, and dried meat, along with bundled strips of dried pumpkin. Braided corn of white, yellow, red, and purple hung from the roof poles, along with dried roots and herbs, forming colorful patterns against the dark elm bark.

The longhouses were kept neat and tidy. With so many people living together, they had to keep their possessions out of the way. The longhouse was never completely silent. Although people spent most of their time outdoors, there was usually someone at home. Many people kept dogs, which roamed about the longhouse or rested in their own sleeping places. Day and night, someone tended a simmering kettle of stew. Any resident as well as visitors from other houses were welcome to help themselves. Rules of behavior ensured order and relative privacy. Families were expected to keep their part of the house clean, keep noise to a minimum, and fix their eyes on the ground as they moved along the longhouse corridor. At the end of the corridor was another storage vestibule and another doorway leading out into the clearing.

CHAPTER FIVE

Communities

Settlements

Woodlands people chose the sites for their settlements carefully. The villages had to be near water—a clear stream for drinking water, a navigable river or lake for transportation, and good fishing places. The site needed to be close to stands of trees for building and firewood. Most people preferred to build their villages, and even temporary settlements, at beautiful locations. They usually chose a spot on high ground, which gave them a pleasing view as well as protection against attack. The ground needed to be level with good farming soil nearby. A good site might also have a hill or copse of trees to shield the village from the cold north wind. Many villages appeared along the coast to take advantage of the rich shellfish beds and coastal fishing areas.

Settlements varied in size from small clusters of five to fifteen lodges to villages of fifty or more buildings. Within the village, structures might be from 20 to 100 feet long and include single-fire and multiple-family dwellings. An average of six hundred people lived in a village, but some held thousands. The villages expanded as families grew and groups banded together, occasionally reaching two hundred structures with about four thousand residents.

Sometimes houses were built around an open space that served as a central plaza for feasts and ceremonies. In some villages, the houses were arranged in rows like streets. Feasts would take place on the central street, and dances and rituals were performed in a small area surrounded by carved posts. If built near a river, the houses might surround a public square on three sides, with the river as the fourth side. In other settlements, the houses were randomly placed. Bark sheds were attached to or placed near many dwellings. The chief's house might be somewhat larger than the other lodges. Often a large structure was used for a council chamber, village ceremonies, and other gatherings.

Villages were busy places full of people. Much of the daily work was done outdoors whenever possible. Women ground their corn with their babies propped on cradle-boards beside them. Groups of children played nearby. Men sat together on the ground, chipping flint into arrow-heads. Although people laughed and talked as they worked, villages were rather quiet.

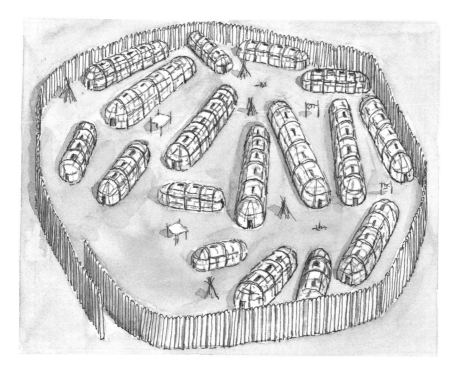

Villages were usually kept quite clean. In some, men dug large garbage pits, which were lined and covered with bark and grass. In others, refuse could be taken outside the settlement and thrown over an embankment.

Many people protected their villages by surrounding them with walls of timber 15 to 20 feet high. These palisades ranged from single fences of thick, pointed logs to elaborate double or triple walls with leaning posts inserted to support balconies from which the villagers hurled rocks and shot arrows at attackers. Stockades usually overlapped at the entrance, forming a fenced passageway into the village.

Tremendous quantities of wood were used to build houses and palisades, and a constant supply was needed to feed the fires that were kept burning in the lodges. An average of 7 to 15 acres had to be cleared to supply the

wood for a stockaded village. A large village for thousands of individuals might require 40 to 50 acres of woodland.

After a decade or two, there were not enough nearby stands of saplings for house and stockade repairs and additions. Firewood and roofing bark became scarce, and the forest game was depleted. The soil became exhausted. The accumulation of refuse and invasions of fleas made the town unlivable. When a decision was reached to abandon the village, the whole community moved together. The bark structures would be left to decay, and the group would relocate on a new site.

Families and Kinships

Community and kinship were the foundations of Indian life. It was very difficult for an individual to break these ties and move to another village. Within a family and a community, each person was involved in a set of relationships that controlled every aspect of his or her life. Each family of parents and children usually had its own hearth; this was the fireside family. An extended family of grandparents, aunts, uncles, and cousins often lived in the same house. The sisters of a child's mother were also considered that child's mothers, and the child's cousins were "brothers" and "sisters." Children also often had a close relationship with their mother's brother or father.

Each person was born into a clan. In many groups a child belonged to his or her mother's clan. The head of the clan, or Clan Matron, was usually the oldest or most respected member of the clan. Any member of the clan was considered a relative. Relationships extended to other villages and other tribes. Since such a large group of people were considered relatives, everyone had many people to turn to for help. Sharing was expected and practiced.

Clans were often grouped into larger divisions that were spoken of as "groups of sisters and brothers." Usually there were two groups of clans in each tribe. Each group had a separate role in councils, ceremonies, and funerals and formed opposing teams for games.

Each sex had well-defined duties and responsibilities. The clearing was the domain of women. Women controlled the household and its resources, the stores of food, and the fields. They cultivated and gathered plants, processed, stored, and cooked the food, kept the fire going, and made the clothing. Occasionally women hunted small game and birds and frequently helped to butcher and bring back the game.

The forest was the domain of men. Men protected the tribe and family and provided meat and skins. Men did most of the fishing, but some women also liked to fish. Men helped with the heavy labor of chopping down trees, clearing the fields, cutting bark, and any aspect of building that required strength. Men and women shared the work on many big jobs—harvesting, maple sugaring, and building canoes.

Marriage was arranged by the women of both families. People belonging to the same clan could not marry. Proposals were often made by the man offering a gift, which the woman could accept or refuse. There was no wedding ceremony. In many societies, the couple would live with the wife's family. In some groups they lived with whichever family had room. Marriage was usually permanent. Divorce was possible, but great efforts were made to patch up a marriage before the couple was allowed to separate.

When a baby was born, the father made a cradleboard,

a flat, smooth carrier about 2 to 3 feet long and about a foot wide. The infant was wrapped in skins and strapped to the board. The child's covering was filled with a soft pad of cattail or milkweed fluff, duck feathers, or sphagnum moss, which prevented chafing and was used for diapers. The mother carried the cradleboard on her back wherever she went. While she was grinding corn or working in the field, she leaned the board against a tree or hung it on a nearby

branch. If a mother didn't have enough milk, she would feed her child a thin paste made of crushed hickory nuts.

Young children stayed close to their mothers, playing and working together. They did not have formal schools, but learned by observing and helping. They helped their mothers plant, watched the fields, gathered food in the woods, memorized tribal legends, and learned the arts and skills they would need later. When they were eight or nine years old, they began to take separate paths toward their adult roles. Girls learned to cook and sew and do other household tasks. Boys formed groups that played at hunting and war. Children were taught the skills that they would use as grown men or women.

When a child reached adolescence, it was often customary to go into the forest alone on a vision quest. He or she would fast in a hut, hoping to have a vision and acquire a guardian spirit. When a girl returned, she went back to helping her mother. When a boy returned, his relationship with his father became closer, and he began to participate in the hunt.

When a person died, the members of the opposite clan buried the dead and helped console the grieving family.

Burial customs differed from tribe to tribe. Bodies were buried in graves or set on a scaffolding. Most people believed that the soul journeyed to an afterlife, although it might visit its former body. Gifts of pelts and equipment were placed with the dead, since the soul required the same things that were needed in life. Many tribes had ceremonies in which people from neighboring villages brought the bones of relatives and put them together in a common grave. As the people lived together in unity, so the remains of loved ones were united in the same place.

Food

Finding and preparing food occupied a large part of the lives of woodlands people. Farming, hunting, fishing, and gathering provided their food supply. The people called the corn, beans, and squash grown in their fields "the three sisters" and "our supporters." Together they made up a balanced diet and also provided a sure source of food that could be stored through the long winter. As farming became more dependable and accounted for a larger portion of food, the people could stay longer in one place, build bigger villages, expand their population, and live a more secure life. For some groups, food produced by farming made up about half of their total diet. No group, however, wanted to give up entirely the patterns of work and travel and the variety of foods that were part of their seasonal rounds.

People seldom ate more than one regular meal a day and never more than two. The women cooked a meal in the morning. During the day, they kept the leftover food in an egg-shaped clay pot that was propped with stones over a low fire. Anyone who felt hungry could ladle some of the stew into a wooden bowl and eat it with a wooden spoon. If a hunter was expected home in the evening, the woman might cook another meal. A good housekeeper always had a pot of warm food for family and guests, and women shared their food generously with neighbors and strangers.

A woman spent part of her day preparing flour and meal. She knew which nuts, fruits, and berries needed processing to remove toxins and how to store foodstuffs that could be ground or milled. She put dried food into her mortar, which was a hollowed-out section of a tree trunk,

and pounded it with a wooden or stone pestle. Meal was sifted in loosely woven baskets. The woman also had a stone bowl and round stone for grinding smaller quantities.

Women knew many ways to cook foods and used great ingenuity in preparing meals. Fresh food was barbecued directly over the fire. Porridges and stews could be boiled in a clay or stone pot. If a woman did not have a fireproof pot, water could be boiled and food cooked in bark pots or tightly woven baskets by plunging red-hot stones into the liquid. Women broiled some food over hot coals. They baked cornbread and berry cakes by wrapping them in leaves or bark and placing them in a hole in the ground with hot ashes. The hole was covered with earth and the food left to cook overnight.

They used a wide variety of foods and combined them in different ways. To prepare a stew, a woman boiled corn, beans, or pumpkin in water, adding pieces of fresh, smoked, or dried meat or fish with roots or vegetables. The Indians ate every kind of animal except flesh-eaters, like wolves.

Pots were wiped out with grasses to clean them. Washing spoiled the pot's finish and was avoided if possible. If something burned or stuck in a pot, or if it began to smell strong, the woman washed it in the river, scrubbing it with rushes and using sand as scouring powder.

In this rich environment, famines were rare, since there were enough wild foods to eat when crops failed or were destroyed by enemies. People enjoyed a healthful, diverse diet. They had strong bones and little tooth decay, and debilitating diseases caused by malnutrition were extremely rare. The Indians were known for their strength and endurance. They could miss meals if necessary without a great loss of stamina. The diet of the people of the woodlands was well-balanced and satisfied every nutritional need.

Clothing

Clothing usually came from animal skins, although some garments were woven from plant fibers. Women prepared skins by first soaking them under water. Next the skins were scraped and rubbed with a paste of the animal's own liver and brains. Then they were dried and rubbed with polished wood until they were soft and pliable. When she was ready to make new clothes, a woman cut the skins on a wooden board with a flint knife and used a bone awl and needle for sewing.

In warm weather, the men and boys wore only a breechcloth, a piece of fringed deerskin about 4 feet long and a foot wide. A deerskin thong was tied around the waist, and the breechcloth was passed between the legs, under the belt, and draped in front and back like an apron. Cloaks were designed so that the left arm was covered but the right arm was free to use a bow and arrow. Leggings were tied to the waist belt in cold weather. The people conditioned themselves to withstand most cold weather without heavy clothing. In warm weather, women and girls wore skirts that went from the waist to a little below the knees. They added overdresses, leggings, and cloaks in cold weather. Small children wore nothing at all in the summer and skins and furs in the winter. Everyone protected their feet with moccasins. Clothes for ceremonies and special occasions were beautifully decorated with porcupine quills, dyes, shells, and beads.

Art and Technology

Indian women were artists with birch bark and twine, adept at making many articles of convenience and beauty. Cutting, folding, and sewing pieces of bark, they fashioned buckets, pots, dishes, and baskets in which they carried, cooked, and stored the family's food and possessions. By scraping the dark layers of bark or attaching small pieces of bark and quills, they decorated their containers with pictures of plants and animals. They also wove mats and baskets from a variety of vegetable fibers and made small baskets that they hung from their waists to carry seeds or food. Loosely woven baskets were used for sifting and tightly woven baskets could hold water.

Women also made strong pottery out of powdered shell mixed with clay, that could be used to boil water and that didn't break even if the water boiled away. Some women rolled the clay into strips, adding one above the other as they shaped and rounded their pots. Others took a lump of clay and hollowed the center with their fist, shaping and smoothing with the other hand. Pots were decorated with incised designs.

Women made cornhusk dolls for their children, often with carefully sewn and decorated clothes.

Men worked in wood. By charring, carving, and rubbing, they created beautiful bowls, dishes, spoons, and utensils. Sometimes they carved animal figures into the handles. The men also made all their tools and weapons, using wood, stone, and bone.

The Indians made fires by twirling a stick of hardwood about the length of an arrow in the socket of a piece of dry softwood, rubbing the rod rapidly between their palms

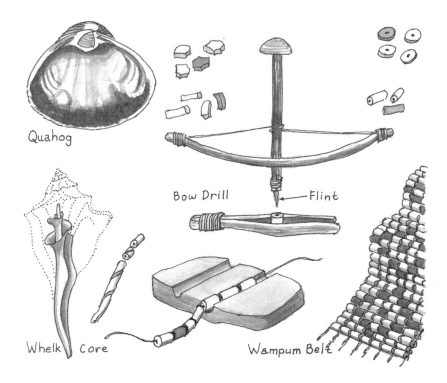

Quahog

Bow Drill   Flint

Whelk   Core   Wampum Belt

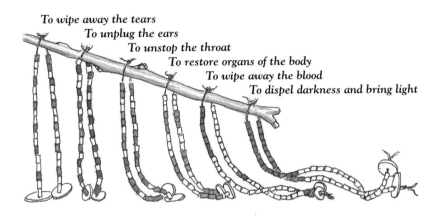

To wipe away the tears
To unplug the ears
To unstop the throat
To restore organs of the body
To wipe away the blood
To dispel darkness and bring light

These words are taken from the Requickening Address which comforts the grieving and symbolically restores life. Each message is accompanied by a string of wampum.

until the wood dust in the socket started to smoke. Then they ignited it with tinder of dry wood or shredded cedar bark.

Men also made musical instruments, such as wooden drums with skin drumheads, carved flutes, and rattles fashioned from gourds, horns, and turtle shells filled with beans or pebbles.

Purple and white shell beads, known as wampum, were strung together and sewn onto belts, ornaments, and jewelry. Valued as money, ornaments, and gifts, they also had many ceremonial purposes and were given as tokens of agreement and seals of friendship. Strings of wampum were sometimes picked up to begin a ceremony and put down to signify the end, or held in turn by speakers. They were also used to keep records and remind speakers of the order and wording of rituals.

Recreation

Both children and adults played a wide variety of games and sports. Some were played outdoors, some were quiet games played in the lodge, and some brought together people from many villages. Running, swimming, and marksmanship competitions were often held. The people especially enjoyed gambling games, betting strings of wampum, furs, and other valuables. Some players lost all the clothes they were wearing, betting on a match. During ceremonies and on certain other occasions, games took on a spiritual significance. Sometimes they became part of a ritual to cure illness or restore balance within the community. Rough sports like lacrosse were one of the few outlets for anger in a society based on cooperation, and they played an important part in Indian life. Even in these games, however, the emphasis was on a team's victory rather than individual glory.

The Indians' lacrosse was similar to the modern version of the game. It was played with a wood or leather ball and long hickory sticks bent at one end and covered with a net of sinews. Two poles were placed as gateways at each end of the playing field. Each team tried to carry or drive the ball through its opponent's gate. Hands must never touch the ball. If it fell to the ground, a player had to lift it with his stick. Lacrosse was often played by hundreds of players on a field a mile long.

Snow snakes was a popular winter game. The object was to see which player or team could throw the snow snake—a tapered rod 5 to 9 feet long—the farthest along a track. The track was made by pulling a log over a path as long as two or three football fields and sprinkling the path with water to form an icy surface. Good players could send the stick gliding 100 to 250 yards.

The Bowl Game was a game of chance played by opposing sides. Six peach or plum pits were placed in a bowl. Each pit was burned black on one side. A player hit the bowl against a bench or the floor, causing the stones to

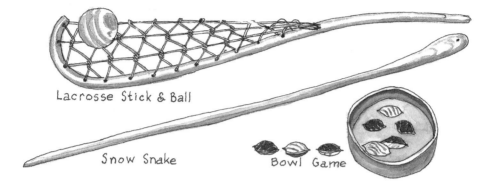

Lacrosse Stick & Ball

Snow Snake

Bowl Game

jump. If five or six of the stones fell with the same color up, the player scored and could take another turn. The scoring system, kinds of bets, counters used, players, and the occasions for the game varied from group to group.

It is said that the Bowl Game was taught to the Iroquois people by Deganawidah, a legendary hero and one of the founders of the Iroquois Confederacy. In Native American society, games were fun, exciting, and played with enthusiasm, but they often had a serious purpose. Teams held secret meetings to work out their own set of songs, objects, and charms for power or luck. The dreams of the players might contain messages about how to play the game successfully. The Bowl Game could be played to cure someone who was sick. The harder the game was played, the better the medicine. The game was also part of important agricultural ceremonies—the Planting Festival, the Green Corn Ceremony, and the Harvest Festival—where it became a religious act symbolizing the struggle of the crops. Stones turning upright represented fertile fields and a plentiful crop. Among some people it was played to predict the abundance of certain crops. For example, if one team won, it signified a large pumpkin crop; if the other won, berries would be plentiful.

Festivals and Work

While each time of the year had its work, it also had its festivals, which gave religious meaning to the work. The Indians believed that all living things had responsibilities toward one another. Harmony and balance were more important than the triumph of good over evil. To keep the world in balance, all creatures had to play out their assigned roles faithfully. They believed the people had to perform rituals to keep the world going. Otherwise, crops would not flourish, the hunt would not be successful, and the world would die. The festivals were held when work could be interrupted or when a natural pause occurred. Most groups had ceremonies that the entire tribe took part in as well as secret rituals that only members of a special society were allowed to perform.

Ceremonies usually began and ended with prayers of thanksgiving to show gratitude for the bounty the people had been given. People recited traditional speeches and stories about the ceremony. Other parts involved burning the sacred tobacco to carry the prayers skyward, songs, dances, feasting, and games. Special costumes and masks were often worn.

The most important ceremony of the year was the Midwinter Festival at the end of the hunting season, a time of little activity for the people. It was the longest of all the ceremonies, lasting about a week. Many rituals were performed as the people gave thanks to the Creator for the continued existence of all things and looked back over the past year and forward to the year that was to come.

During the days of the Dream Guessing Rite, people tried to clear their minds of old dreams for a fresh start in

Basswood

the new year. People in opposite clans guessed each other's dreams. A person who had a troubling dream would hint at the subject of his dream in the form of riddles. "It whistles in the wind" might refer to the corn spirit. "It has holes, yet it catches" would be a lacrosse stick. If a dream was especially hard to guess, everyone would struggle to get the answer, because it was essential that the dream be guessed. When someone finally came up with the right answer, the people would cheer. The person who guessed correctly promised to make a protective charm for the dreamer, a miniature of the object he had guessed, or to give the dreamer a gift of food.

Each person sang a personal song. The song belonged only to that person and renewed the strength of the guardian spirit whose magical power protected him or her.

Sometimes when a person was sick, a medicine society was called on to perform curing rituals. The False Face Society wore special masks when performing their rites. Once cured, the individual had to renew the cure by having the same ritual performed at the Midwinter Festival, an occasion for each individual to set things right in his or her connection with the world.

The Maple Ceremony, the first festival of the spring, was held when the sap ran in the maple trees. It gave thanks to the maple, to the forest, and to the Creator for the gift of both. The people also prayed that the trees swaying in the high winds would not shed their boughs on human settlements. The day-long ceremonies included dancing, games, and burning the sacred tobacco and ended with a feast.

After the women had planted the seeds, the people held a Planting Festival. It also lasted a day and was celebrated in much the same way as the Maple Festival.

When the strawberries ripened in the spring, the people gave thanks in a Strawberry Ceremony, ending with a feast of the fresh berries.

Later in the year, when the string beans ripened in the fields, a day was set aside to give thanks for the beans in the Green Bean Ceremony.

The Green Corn Ceremony was held in the late summer, when the corn was ready to eat. It was a longer ceremony, lasting three to four days, and honored the Creator and the Corn Mother, who gave the people the first corn. The whole community could rejoice, knowing that the crops would be good. Children born since midwinter were named then. The clans had a store of names that held certain characteristics. By giving the child that name, he or she would become the kind of person that fit the name. Speeches were made and the Thanksgiving Address given, followed by the Feather Dance, one of the most important and most beautiful of all the ceremonial dances. Sacred tobacco was burned and other dances held. Then the people played games and concluded the day with a feast of corn soup. The daylight rituals were quiet and solemn, but in the evening there were lively social dances, and people danced and sang late into the night. The festival ended with the playing of the Bowl Game.

When the harvest was gathered and the people were

assured of food for the long winter to come, they held a Harvest Festival to honor "the three sisters," corn, beans, and squash. This also lasted four days and was similar to the Green Corn Festival. The ceremonial food was succotash, a mixture of beans and corn. With the Harvest Festival, the agricultural part of the year was brought to an end.

Warfare

Warfare served many purposes in the tribal culture. It was first and foremost a ritual, a rite of passage into manhood. Every man was expected to be a warrior, and it was an opportunity for them to test their bravery and gain prestige. A war was frequently fought to get revenge. Families of a man who had been slain gave presents to the war chief to encourage him to lead an attack against the tribe of the slayer. At times war was an economic necessity. People suffering scarcity raided others for food or seized captives to replace a population that had suffered losses from disease. Sometimes a war was fought to protect hunting territories or trade routes that were being used by other tribes. War was an important outlet for pent-up anger and hostility; anger, which could not be shown at home, could safely be turned on enemies.

When a war chief wanted to attack another tribe, he might spread rumors of enemy sightings to gain support among the people. A war council would be held to decide to go to war and make plans for attacking and raiding. Before the war party left, the people held a war feast. They sang and danced and sought the support of supernatural spirits.

Each warrior carried a bag of cornmeal that would last until he returned. If a war party went out in several sections, the first would leave marks on a tree at a trail crossing to indicate who was in the party. Sometimes they painted clan symbols on the tree, with the number of warriors present from each clan. The men fought with bows and arrows and wooden clubs. They often wore armor made of wooden slats carefully bound together and carried wooden shields. This armor was usually able to stop arrows. If the men were traveling by canoe, they used the canoes as shields and as ladders to climb palisade walls.

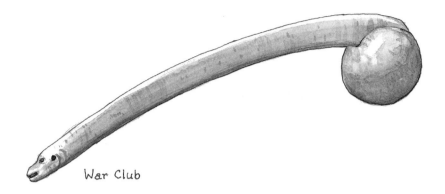
War Club

Warriors were cruel to their enemies, and prisoners were brutally tortured. Occasionally a family would adopt a prisoner to replace a dead relative, but most prisoners could expect to die. Fierce fighting and the merciless treatment of captives were methods of defense, making other tribes afraid.

A war post usually stood in the village, painted with a pictorial record of its wars. It was a story of men killed and prisoners taken, of the campaigns that the men fought and the plunder they brought back from their raids.

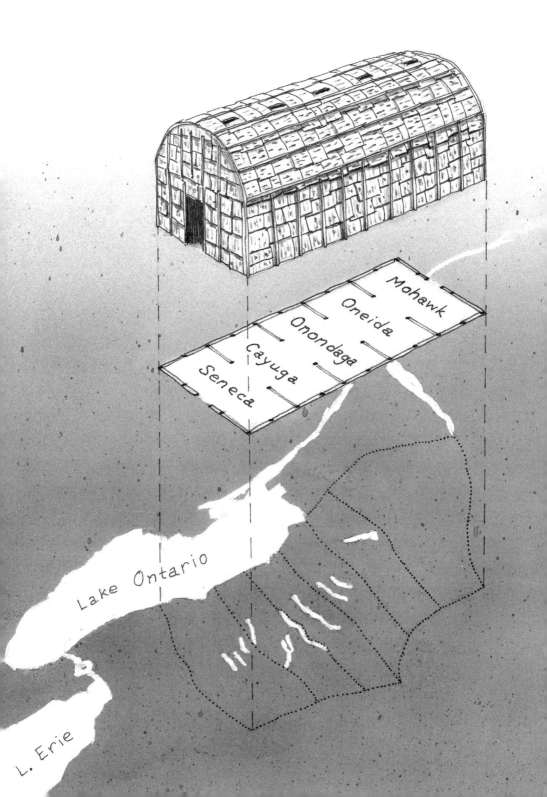

Mohawk

Oneida

Onondaga

Cayuga

Seneca

Lake Ontario

L. Erie

CHAPTER SIX

Political Organization

Tribes

The basic political unit was the tribe. A chief governed each tribe, his power varying with its customs. Some chiefs were absolute rulers, some served more as important advisers. No matter how powerful, a chief seldom exercised his authority in important matters without holding a council, and he listened carefully to his advisers. Elders were respected and their opinions valued when tribal issues were discussed. Women were included in the councils of many tribes; they were regarded as having experience and good judgment. Public opinion was an important factor. Usually a chief tried to reach a decision agreeable to everyone and took the time necessary to succeed. The eloquence of a speaker had great influence and often swayed opinion. Proper consideration might take hours or even days before a decision was reached.

Chiefs came to power in different ways. In some tribes, the chief inherited his position. In other tribes, the position was related to a man's character, accomplishments, and prestige, as well as his ability to command respect. Among some people, a woman could become chief if her husband died. Sometimes a woman was chosen when there was no suitable member of the male line. The women of some tribes chose the chiefs and had the power to remove them from office.

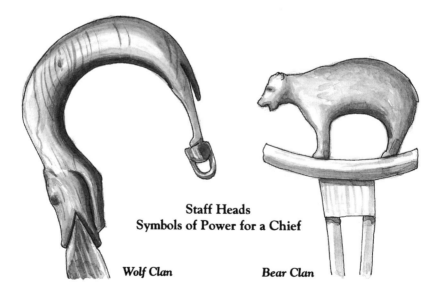

**Staff Heads
Symbols of Power for a Chief**

Wolf Clan   *Bear Clan*

Tribal territories did not have fixed borders. Boundaries changed with movement among the tribes. Yet at any given time there was a general understanding of defining natural landmarks and resources that were used exclusively by a particular group.

Confederacies

Some woodlands tribes joined to form confederacies—the Iroquois Confederacy, the Huron League, the Petun or Tobacco League, the Neutrals, the Erie, the Abenaki Confederacy, and the Powhatan Confederacy. Tribal nations were united in a confederacy by their common interests and common enemies. The Huron formed a league of four nations. They shared a common language, but each retained its own traditions.

The Iroquois Confederacy was a great achievement. The five tribes that dominated the region from the St. Lawrence River to Lake Champlain had long been bitter enemies, and their constant warfare caused death and destruction among all the people. Sometime between 1400 and 1600, two heroes, Deganawidah and Hiawatha, united these tribes—the Seneca, Mohawk, Onondaga, Cayuga, and Oneida. They called themselves Hodenosaunee, "People of the Longhouse." At the famous council that is said to have formed their league, the people were taught how to build a longhouse, which became a symbol of its political and military unity.

The Iroquois spoke of their domain as a gigantic longhouse with five fires that stretched 240 miles in what is now New York State, from Albany to the shore of Lake Erie at Buffalo. Within this symbolic longhouse the tribes had various names, signifying both their geographic location and their kinship ties with one another. The eastern end of the longhouse was guarded by the Mohawk, who were known as "Keepers of the Eastern Door." The Seneca were "Keepers of the Western Door." "Secure the doors" meant for the Mohawk and the Seneca to keep a close watch on their territories. In the center was the territory of the Onondaga, called "Keepers of the Central Fire." Meetings of the great council took place in the fall in Onandaga territory. These three powerful tribes were referred to as "the Elder Brothers." The Cayuga and the

Oneida, smaller and less powerful tribes, were "the Younger Brothers." The central aisle of the symbolic longhouse was the Iroquois Trail, which aided communication and provided mutual defense for the league. In the Confederacy, the Iroquois people saw the familiar relationships of their daily lives carried out on a larger scale. The sixth nation, the Tuscarora, did not join the others until the early eighteenth century.

CHAPTER SEVEN
Other Structures

The Conical Wigwam

Across northern New England and southern Canada, the
Penobscot, Micmac, Naskapi, and other tribes built conical, bark-covered wigwams framed with straight poles. In
the northern reaches of the woodlands, there were not
enough days without frost to grow maize successfully. The
people lived by hunting, fishing, and gathering and built
lodges similar to those of the hunters of the Great Plains.

They began construction by cutting poles about 14 feet
long of cedar, spruce, or fir, leaving the bark intact. The
builder lashed the tops of four poles together, positioning
their bases evenly around the circular floor plan. The
remaining poles filled in the circle, their tops resting in
the crotches where the four poles joined. A horizontal ring

of small branches was tied near the midsection to stabilize the cone. In very cold weather, insulating grass was layered over the frame; then the birchbark sheets were tied on. Additional poles supported the structure's exterior and were bound together at the top to keep the bark sheets in place.

Inside the lodge, the women built a fireplace in the center and laid a flooring of fresh fir boughs around the hearth. Space in these houses had to be used with extreme efficiency. All the tools, supplies, and equipment had a place; some were hung from the poles and bars. If two families lived together, the wigwam could be extended with a ridge pole. The conical wigwam was a simple, sturdy structure, well suited for people who moved to follow game.

The Sweat House

Sweat bathing was a cleansing and prayer ritual practiced throughout Indian America in a special domed wigwam about 6 feet in diameter and 4 feet high. It was constructed outside the palisades or a short distance from the village, usually at the edge of a stream or river. The frame was encased in bark or mats so that steam could not escape. Rocks were heated to a glowing red in a large fire nearby. These stones were then carried into the lodge and placed in a pit in the center. With the participants huddled inside, a leader ladled water over the hot rocks, filling the hut with hissing steam. Bathers prayed and sang as they were cleansed by the steam. At the end of the ritual, they rubbed themselves with sand and plunged into the cold stream to refresh and renew their bodies and spirits.

The Field Watcher's Hut

Fields and gardens on the outskirts of the village were guarded during the growing season. Birds and other animals could destroy crops, and an enemy attack could endanger the winter's food supply. Sometimes the villagers watched the fields from a special hut. Four forked posts were placed at the corners to hold support poles. Planks were laid across the poles to form a platform overlooking the fields. A lean-to, tent, or hut was built on the platform

to shade the watcher, who chased birds away and looked for the approach of an enemy.

The Shaking Tent

The smallest building, used by the Chippewa and other groups across the woodlands, was known as "the shaking tent" or "conjuring lodge." It was about the size of a phone booth and had a bent sapling frame made from specially harvested poles. The Chippewa used three birch and three spruce frame poles with two birch and two spruce horizontal saplings to bind them together. Although other tribes used different kinds of poles, construction was the same. Saplings were planted deep in the ground and angled

slightly outward to give the building added strength. Rattles of caribou and deer hooves were tied to the frame.

A shaman performed a special ritual in this lodge to find answers to questions troubling the people of the tribe. Where was game? When would the rains come? When would they stop? Were enemies nearby? After the shaman stepped inside, the frame was covered with bark. He then called on a supernatural helper to bring him answers. Eerie voices and noises came from the lodge, and it swayed and shook violently. The Indians believed that in the shaking tent, the shaman could make contact between the human world and the world of the spirits.

CHAPTER EIGHT
Travel

Traveling over Land

Footpaths crossed the woodlands in all directions, deeply worn from centuries of travel. Trails connected Indian villages with their fields, fishing places, maple sugaring groves, hunting grounds, and all the sites of their seasonal rounds. They also connected one clearing with another for trade and communication between villages. The people found the fastest, easiest, and most practical ways to travel. They crossed streams and rivers at the shallowest and safest places or where the waterway could be bridged by felling a single tree. Routes were chosen for available springs and dry, safe camping places. Swamps and steep terrain were avoided. Large boulders became mortars where travelers could grind food.

Most trails were narrow, only 1 or 2 feet wide and 3 to 12 inches deep, but they might be worn 2 feet deep in places where they were heavily traveled. The Indians did not need a wide road, because they generally walked single file. The paths were clear enough for runners; messengers could cover 30 to 50 miles in a single day.

The great Iroquois Trail stretched "from fire to fire," connecting the villages of the Five Nations. A network of paths crossing other parts of their land branched from the central trail. The trail helped the people keep in touch and maintain their unity, and there was a good deal of visiting among villages and nations. The trails were so well

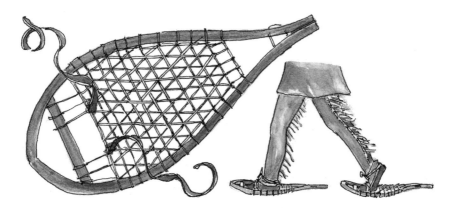

chosen that many roads in New York State today follow the old trails.

Snowshoes were used for transportation in the winter. These shoes were constructed of wooden frames, crossed with netting and brace pieces. They were held on by thongs and had an opening to let the toe move below the shoe surface as the heel went up in the act of walking. Depending on their availability, white ash, hickory, cedar, and beech were preferred for the frames. The wood was steamed and bent into a variety of shapes. Different styles were associated with each tribe.

Traveling over Water

To travel on waterways, the Indians of the woodlands built light, portable, bark-covered canoes, skillfully made with only stone tools. These canoes were strong and stable. They were built in various sizes to hold two to twenty men and their supplies, and they did not easily capsize even in rough waters. Since they were paddled, not rowed, the people faced the direction they were going. This was

Black Spruce
gum for sealing seams

Cedar
for frame and ribs

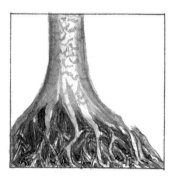

Black Spruce
roots for sewing pieces

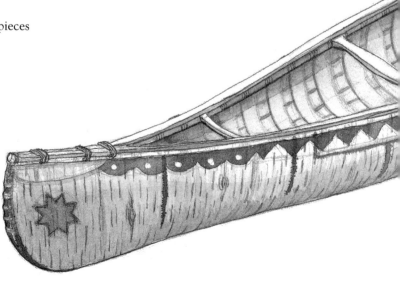

Maple
for paddle and crosspieces

Birch
for cover

Birchbark Canoe

important in steering through treacherous waters. The canoes were fast, easy to handle, and could skim through shallow waters. Since they were made of materials that were plentiful, it was simple to make repairs. The canoes of each tribe had a distinctive style.

Builders used the best materials that were available nearby. The bark of many species of trees was used to make canoes, but the smooth outer bark of white or paper birch was generally regarded as the best. Sheets of bark were peeled from chosen trees in the spring. If construction was not to begin immediately, these fragile sheets were rolled and submerged in a nearby stream or lake to keep them pliable.

The long, thin roots of the black spruce were used as thread to sew the seams. These roots were tough, durable, and flexible. They grew close to the surface and were easily pulled from the soft soil by hand or with a stick. As soon as they were harvested, they were split with a sharp stone, coiled, and kept in water until needed.

The Indians used spruce gum to seal the seams and make them watertight. During the winter, the builder cut notches in the trunks of spruce trees; in the spring he would scrape the resin from the scars and also collect it from damaged or fallen trees. The sticky resin would be heated before it was applied to all the seams.

The frame of the canoe was made of cedar, spruce, maple, or ash. Cutting and shaping the wooden pieces was slow work with stone tools. The ribs were bent by soaking them in boiling water.

In addition to gathering materials, it was necessary to select a building site with a smooth, shady area free of stones and roots. It also needed to be a good campsite, with food and water easily available, because construction took a long time and involved the whole family. The same sites were used by generations of Indians. The men cut the trees, stripped the bark, gathered the gum, and built the frames. Sewing the sheets of bark together and lashing the pieces onto the frame was the work of the women.

CHAPTER NINE
The Clash of Cultures

The coming of the white settlers changed the lives of the native people forever. When they first met, the Indians, for the most part, welcomed and helped the strangers. They provided them with food and shelter and guided them through the land, often enabling them to survive and succeed.

However, their encounters soon became a series of conflicts, with each group trying to drive the other away. The central issue was usually land, with the growing white population always needing more and the native people watching their territories dwindle through invasions, forced sales, trickery, and the violation of treaties. All the motives Europeans had for coming to America, no matter how noble, would be served at the expense of the native people. Even in a continent of such vast land and resources, there was not enough for all.

The fur trade had a disastrous impact on the Woodland Indians. Their seasonal round of hunting and fishing was disrupted as they spent more time and energy trapping small game and trading the pelts for kettles, knives, hatchets, bells, and cloth. Farming also suffered as the Indian women spent more time processing beaver and other animal skins. Each tribe tried to gain an advantage in what had become the most important source of wealth in the region. These intense trade rivalries eventually strained confederacies and turned friendly tribes against one another. The balance between the Indians and their environment shifted. New products changed the materials the people used in their daily lives, and they were no longer self-sufficient. The Woodland Indians, who had once hunted only for food and clothing, began to hunt for material gain. Killing large numbers of game, neglecting their farms, and disrupting their cycle of work caused starvation and death in many tribes. The Indians now had few ways to provide for themselves other than selling their land.

For a long time after the Indians and Europeans met, neither understood what "selling" land meant to the other. The Indians believed that they were granting permission for the use of the land, not giving up their own hunting and fishing rights. They were happy to collect goods for granting this use. To the white settlers, however, it meant a permanent transfer, after which they alone could use the land for whatever they pleased. The loss of their territory was devastating to the Indians; to lose their land was to lose their way of life.

As regular contact between the cultures increased, disease spread. Epidemics of typhoid fever, diphtheria, measles, chicken pox, whooping cough, tuberculosis, and other illnesses previously unknown to the Indians spread through their communities. This proved to be one of the most devastating aspects of the encounters with Europeans. Entire Indian populations died from these diseases. As the number of Native Americans dwindled, immigrants were pouring into America from Europe.

The conversion to Christianity by missionaries created more rifts within Indian society. When the missionaries were successful, entire tribes ceased to exist as distinct political and cultural groups.

Indian tribes allied themselves with white people in their conflicts with each other. Intertribal feuds, which had been going on for generations, seemed stronger than their shared identity as a people. Many Indian leaders saw the need for unified action and attempted to convince the tribes to work together, but they were never able to attain their goals.

The history of America's growth and expansion is the history of the Indians' displacement. Even against the white man's superior weapons, Indians proved to be some of the world's most effective warriors. However, they were defeated by overwhelming numbers, devastating diseases, and their own lack of unity. Eventually the people were scattered on small reservations in the United States and Canada.

As vacant land filled with settlers, the Indians were completely shut out of their hunting grounds. They had little access to the resources of the forest and little land left to sell. Since they could no longer move when the soil wore out, they had to change their methods of agriculture. Farming became a small family endeavor. The large cooperative community was not appropriate to their lifestyle anymore. The women continued to be important as farmers, but men no longer had their traditional jobs and ways to gain honor.

As the Indian culture and way of life seemed to be vanishing in the early nineteenth century, a Seneca prophet, Handsome Lake, helped reaffirm and adapt the best of the traditional beliefs. He revived the longhouse as a symbol of unity. His followers met in a rectangular meeting hall built of logs with a gable roof. This longhouse was used for religious ceremonies, as a meeting place for tribal discussion, as a dance center and feast hall, and as a schoolhouse where the young were taught the traditional ways.

Even though the work associated with the traditional ceremonies had ceased, they could still be celebrated to reinforce the important themes of thanksgiving, respect for nature, and a fundamental sense of community. The people adapted their code of behavior to their new roles. Now farming was not just women's work, and the bond between husband and wife became stronger.

CHAPTER TEN

The People and the Land Today

Today the great woodlands have been cut down. The wilderness is gone, many of the animals have disappeared, and the indigenous plants have been replaced by cultivated fields. Yet many native people have managed to keep much of their old culture alive despite the strong pressures to forsake it. Some are still living on reservations, the remnants of their ancient lands, rather than seeking a new life elsewhere. They are still governed by councils of chiefs and are following traditional ways.

Some people have found new ways to use their skills. Mohawk men have become famous for their daring construction work on the high frames of skyscrapers and huge bridges. They were attracted to the challenge and danger of work that offered a test of their bravery.

Some people are keeping their culture alive far from their traditional homelands. Four hundred years ago, the Kickapoo were a typical Algonquian woodland people, living in wigwams of sapling frames and woven mats in southern Wisconsin. In escaping the encroachment of white people, their migrations eventually led them to Kansas, Oklahoma, Texas, and northern Mexico, where they still live in small scattered settlements, keeping many of their old customs and building traditional wigwams with frames of cypress or juniper and covers of cane mats or pieces of cardboard. For some modern Chippewa, canvas and tarpaper have replaced cattail mats and bark coverings on their houses. Some huts have concrete floors, with the poles placed in bottles that were set in the wet concrete. In spite of that, their present wigwams look much like those built by their ancestors.

A form of the Iroquois longhouse is still being built and maintained on Iroquois reservations in New York State and southern Ontario. Today they have stud frames, clapboard siding, and shake roofs, but they still house council meetings and ceremonies, and they remain a symbol of unity among the people.

Bibliography

Asterisk (*) indicates books of interest to younger readers.

Adney, Edwin Tappan, and Chapelle, Howard I. *The Bark Canoes and Skin Boats of North America.* Bulletin 230. Washington, D.C.: Smithsonian Institution, 1964.

*"America 1492," *Kids Discover,* vol. 2, no. 7 (August/September 1992).

Beauchamp, William M. *Aboriginal Use of Wood in New York.* Albany: New York State Education Department, 1905. Reprint. New York: AMS Press, 1978.

_____. *Horn and Bone Implements of the New York State Indians.* Albany: University of the State of New York, 1902. Reprint. New York: AMS Press, 1978.

_____. *Wampum and Shell Articles Used by the New York Indians.* Albany: University of the State of New York, 1901. Reprint. New York: AMS Press, 1978.

Blau, Harold. "Dream Guessing: A Comparative Analysis." *Ethnohistory,* vol. 10 (1963): 233–49.

*Bruchac, Joseph. *Children of the Longhouse.* New York: Dial, 1996.

Brundin, Judith A. *The Native People of the Northeast Woodlands.* New York: Museum of the American Indian–Heye Foundation, 1990.

Bushnell, David I., Jr. *Native Villages and Village Sites East of the Mississippi*. Bulletin 69. Washington, D.C.: Smithsonian Institution, 1919.

Caduto, Michael J., and Bruchac, Joseph. *Keepers of Life*. Golden, Colo.: Fulcrum, 1994.

Collins, Beryl Bobichaud, and Anderson, Karl H. *Plant Communities of New Jersey*. New Brunswick, N.J.: Rutgers University Press, 1994.

Connor, Sheila. *New England Natives*. Cambridge, Mass.: Harvard University Press, 1994.

Day, Gordon M. "The Indian as an Ecological Factor in the Northeastern Forest." *Ecology*, vol. 34, no. 2 (April 1953): 329–46.

Driver, Harold E. *Indians of North America*, 2nd ed. Chicago: University of Chicago Press, 1969.

Fichter, George S. *How to Build an Indian Canoe*. New York: David McKay, 1977.

Green, Rayna. *Women in American Indian Society*. Indians of North America Series, general ed. Frank W. Porter III. New York: Chelsea House, 1992.

Grimm, William C. *Indian Harvests*. New York: McGraw-Hill, 1973.

*Harrington, M. R. *The Indians of New Jersey: Dickon Among the Lenapes*. New Brunswick, N.J.: Rutgers University Press, 1966.

*_____. *The Iroquois Trail: Dickon Among the Onondagas and Senecas*. New Brunswick, N.J.: Rutgers University Press, 1965.

Hertzberg, Hazel W. *The Great Tree and the Longhouse*. New York: Macmillan, 1966.

*Hofman, Charles. *American Indians Sing*. New York: John Day, 1967.

*"The Iroquois." *Faces Magazine*, vol. 7, no. 1 (September 1990).

Iroquois Culture, History, and Prehistory. Proceedings of the 1965 Conference on Iroquois Research. Albany: University of New York, 1965.

Josephy, Alvin M. *500 Nations*. New York: Knopf, 1994.

Kinietz, W. Vernon. *The Indians of the Western Great Lakes 1615–1760*. Occasional Contributions from the Museum of Anthropology of the University of Michigan, No. 10. Ann Arbor: University of Michigan Press, 1940.

Kopper, Philip. *The Smithsonian Book of North American Indians*. Washington, D.C.: Smithsonian Institution, 1986.

*LaFarge, Oliver. *A Pictorial History of the American Indian*. New York: Crown, 1956.

Lawrence, Bill. *The Early American Wilderness as the Explorers Saw It*. New York: Paragon House, 1991.

Mangelsdorf, Paul C. *Corn: Its Origin, Evolution, and Improvement.* Cambridge, Mass.: Belknap/Harvard University Press, 1974.

McKusick, Marshall. "Reconstructing the Longhouse Village Settlement Patterns." *Plains Anthropologist*, vol. 19, no. 63 (February 1974): 197–210.

McPhee, John. *The Survival of the Bark Canoe.* New York: Farrar, Straus, and Giroux, 1975.

Minor, Marz Nono. *The American Indian Craft Book.* New York: Popular Library, 1972.

*Monroe, Jean Guard, and Williamson, Ray A. *First Houses: Native American Homes and Sacred Structures.* Boston: Houghton Mifflin, 1993.

Morgan, Lewis Henry. *League of the Iroquois.* Rochester, N.Y.: Sage & Brother, 1851. Reprint. Secaucus, N.J.: Carol, 1996.

Nabokov, Peter, and Easton, Robert. *Native American Architecture.* Oxford, Eng.: Oxford University Press, 1989.

Peattie, Donald Culross. *A Natural History of Trees of Eastern and Central North America.* Boston: Houghton Mifflin, 1964.

*Ridington, Jillian and Robin. *People of the Longhouse.* Buffalo, N.Y.: Firefly Books, 1982.

*_____. *People of the Trail.* Vancouver: Douglas & McIntyre, 1978.

Russell, Howard S. *Indian New England Before the Mayflower*. Hanover, N.H.: University Press of New England, 1980.

*Siegel, Beatrice. *Indians of the Northeast Woodlands*. New York: Walker, 1992.

*Sita, Lisa. *Indians of the Northeast*. New York: Michael Freedman, 1997.

Snow, Dean R. *The Iroquois*. Oxford, Eng.: Blackwell, 1994.

Stites, Sara Henry. *Economics of the Iroquois*. Lancaster, Pa.: New Era, 1905. Reprint. New York: AMS Press, 1978.

Symonds, George W. D. *The Tree Identification Book*. New York: Quill, 1958.

Thomas, David Hurst; Miller, Jay; White, Richard; Nabokov, Peter; and Deloria, Philip J. *The Native Americans*. Atlanta, Ga.: Turner, 1993.

Tooker, Elisabeth. *An Ethnography of the Huron Indians, 1615–1649*. Bureau of American Ethnology, Bulletin 190. Washington, D.C.: Smithsonian Institution, 1964.

———. *Lewis H. Morgan on Iroquois Material Culture*. Tucson: University of Arizona Press, 1994.

Trigger, Bruce G. *The Huron: Farmers of the North*. New York: Holt, Rinehart and Winston, 1969.

_____., ed. *Northeast.* vol. 15, *Handbook of North American Indians,* ed. William C. Sturtevant. Washington, D.C.: Smithsonian Institution, 1978.

Waldman, Carl. *Atlas of the North American Indian.* New York: Facts on File, 1985.

Whitney, Gordon G. *From Coastal Wilderness to Fruited Plain.* Cambridge, Eng.: Cambridge University Press, 1994.

*Wilbur, C. Keith. *Early Explorers of North America.* Chester, Conn.: Globe Pequot, 1989.

*_____. *The New England Indians.* 2nd ed. Old Saybrook, Conn: Globe Pequot, 1996.

Willoughby, Charles C. "Houses and Gardens of the New England Indians." *American Anthropologist,* vol. 8 (1906): 115–32.

Index